LUCY MICKLETHWAIT was born in Quetta, Pakistan, and brought up all over the world; her parents settled in Scotland. She is the author of the highly successful *I Spy* series, which includes *Numbers in Art, An Alphabet of Art, Transport in Art, Shapes in Art* and *Animals in Art*. Her other children's books include *A Child's Book of Art, A Child's Book of Play in Art* and *Discover Great Paintings*. Other titles in the First Art Book series include *Animals: A First Art Book* and *Colours: A First Art Book*. Lucy lives in East London.

For Walter and Molly

First published in Great Britain in 2006 by
Frances Lincoln Children's Books, 4 Torriano Mews
Torriano Avenue, London NW5 2RZ
www.franceslincoln.com

British Library Cataloguing in Publication Data available on request

ISBN 978-1-84507-499-9

Printed in China

1 3 5 7 9 8 6 4 2

Children

A First Art Book

Lucy Micklethwait

F

FRANCES LINCOLN
CHILDREN'S BOOKS

Reading
and writing

learning to read

learning to write

Making music

singing a song

playing a tune

Dancing

learning to dance

dancing in a circle

Riding

riding on a rocking-horse

riding a pony

Swinging

swinging to and fro

swinging round and round

Fishing

fishing in the sea

fishing in a lake

Eating

eating fruit

eating ice-cream

Washing

washing in the bath

washing in a basin

Sleeping

sleeping in the hay

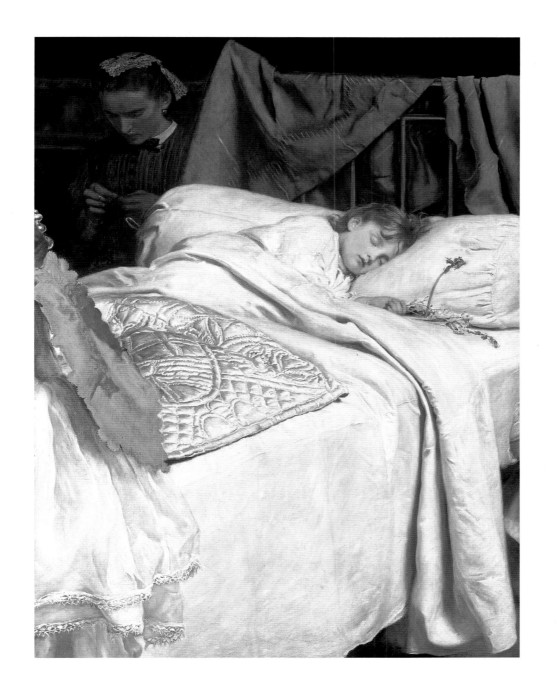

sleeping in bed

Picture List

Reading and writing

learning to read
The Young Schoolmistress (probably 1735–36),
Jean-Siméon Chardin (1699–1779)
Oil on canvas
The National Gallery, London

learning to write
Writing Lesson (1905), Pierre-Auguste Renoir (1841–1919)
Oil on canvas
The Barnes Foundation, Merion, Pennsylvania

Making music

singing a song
O-bon Festival from the series *Children's Games* (1888),
Kobayashi Eitaku (1843–1890)
Woodblock print
Central Saint Martins College of Art and Design, London

playing a tune
The Banjo Lesson (1893), Henry Ossawa Tanner (1859–1937)
Oil on canvas
Hampton University Museum, Hampton, Virginia

Dancing

learning to dance
Dorothea and Francesca (1898), Cecilia Beaux (1855–1942)
Oil on canvas
The Art Institute of Chicago, A.A. Munger Collection

dancing in a circle
Ring Around the Rosie (1910–15), Edward Henry Potthast
(1857–1927)
Oil on canvas
Museum of Fine Arts, Houston, Texas

Riding

riding on a rocking-horse
The Hobby Horse (c.1840), American
Oil on canvas
National Gallery of Art, Washington
Gift of Edgar William and Bernice Chrysler Garbisch

riding a pony
Prince Baltasar Carlos on Horseback (c.1635–36),
Diego Velázquez (1599–1660)
Oil on canvas
The Prado, Madrid

Swinging

swinging to and fro
The Baby Krishna on a Swing (c.1750), Pahari School,
Guler style, India
Gouache on paper
The British Museum, London

swinging round and round
Liberation (1945), Ben Shahn (1898–1969)
Tempera on cardboard mounted on composition board
The Museum of Modern Art, New York, James Thrall Soby Bequest

Fishing

fishing in the sea
Chadding on Mount's Bay (1902), Alexander Stanhope Forbes
(1857–1947)
Oil on canvas
Worcester City Art Gallery and Museum

fishing in a lake
Boy Fishing, Pieter van Slingelandt (1640–1691)
Oil on wood
Gemäldegalerie, Berlin

Eating

eating fruit
Boys eating Melon and Grapes (c.1650), Bartolomé Esteban Murillo
(1617–1682)
Oil on canvas
Alte Pinakothek, Munich

eating ice-cream
Little Girl with Ice-Cream (c.1958), Renato Guttuso (1911–1987)
Oil on canvas
Private Collection

Washing

washing in the bath
Morning [The Artist's Wife and Son] (1910),
Boris Kustodiev (1878–1927)
Oil on canvas
Russian State Museum, St Petersburg

washing in a basin
The Child's Bath (c.1893), Mary Cassatt (1844–1926)
Oil on canvas
The Art Institute of Chicago, Robert A. Waller Fund

Sleeping

sleeping in the hay
Boy Sleeping in the Hay, Albert Anker (1831–1910)
Oil on canvas
Kunstmuseum, Basel

sleeping in bed
Sleeping (c.1865), John Everett Millais (1829–1896)
Oil on canvas
Private Collection

PHOTOGRAPHIC ACKNOWLEDGEMENTS
learning to read: The National Gallery, London/www.bridgeman.co.uk
learning to write: © The Barnes Foundation, Merion,
Pennsylvania/www.bridgeman.co.uk
singing a song: © Central Saint Martins College of Art and Design,
London/www.bridgeman.co.uk
playing a tune: Collection of Hampton University Museum,
Hampton, Virginia
learning to dance: photo © The Art Institute of Chicago (1921.109)
dancing in a circle: Museum of Fine Arts, Houston,
Texas/www.bridgeman.co.uk
riding on a rocking-horse: image © 2006 Board of Trustees,
National Gallery of Art, Washington (1955.11.23)
riding a pony: © photo Scala, Florence
swinging to and fro: © The Trustees of the British Museum
swinging round and round: © Estate of Ben Shahn/VAGA, New York/DACS,
London 2006. © Digital image, The Museum of Modern Art, New York
(1249.1979)/Scala, Florence
fishing in the sea: photo Worcester City Art Gallery and Museum, with kind
permission of the estate of Stanhope Forbes/The Bridgeman Art Library
fishing in a lake: bpk/ Gemäldegalerie, State Museums of Berlin/photo
Jörg P. Anders
eating fruit: © photo Scala, Florence
eating ice-cream: © DACS 2006/© photo Scala, Florence
washing in the bath: © photo Scala, Florence
washing in a basin: photo © The Art Institute of Chicago (1910.2)
sleeping in the hay: Artothek/photo Hans Hinz
sleeping in bed: © Christie's Images Ltd. 2006

OTHER TITLES BY LUCY MICKLETHWAIT FROM FRANCES LINCOLN CHILDREN'S BOOKS

ANIMALS: A FIRST ART BOOK

Here are 18 exciting works of art featuring a range of animals,
from spotty to feathery, and creepy crawly to cuddly. The artists,
chosen from five centuries of art around the world, include
Dürer, Stubbs, Hokusai, Renoir, Warhol and Hockney.
A perfect introduction to art for the very young.

ISBN 978-1-84507-104-2

COLOURS: A FIRST ART BOOK

Here are 18 brilliant works of art carefully chosen to illustrate
a range of familiar colours. Artists include Botticelli, Hiroshige,
and van Gogh and Peter Blake – something new on every page.
A perfect way for the very young to disover great art!

ISBN 978-1-84507-550-7

Frances Lincoln titles are available from all good bookshops.
You can also buy books and find out more about your favourite titles,
authors and illustrators at our website: www.franceslincoln.com